First published by PI Kids as *What Do You See? Around the World.*

**Customer Service: 1-877-277-9441 or CustomerService@PhoenixInternational.com**



Published by PI Kids, an imprint of Phoenix International Publications, Inc.
8501 West Higgins Road    34 Seymour Street    Heimhuder Straße 81
Chicago, Illinois 60631    London W1H 7JE    20148 Hamburg

PI Kids is a trademark of Phoenix International Publications, Inc., and is registered in the United States.

www.PhoenixInternational.com

Library of Congress Control Number: 2024953136

ISBN: 979-8-7654-1209-1

## See and Search

# Around the World

Written by Kathy Broderick

pi kids®
An imprint of PHOENIX International Publications, Inc.
Chicago • London • Hamburg • Mexico City • Sydney

In NEW YORK CITY, there is so much to see.
Find a **taxi**, a **hot dog**, the **Statue of Liberty**,
The **Empire State Building**, the **Subway** too.
Cross the **Brooklyn Bridge**, and enjoy the view!

HOT DOG

Subway

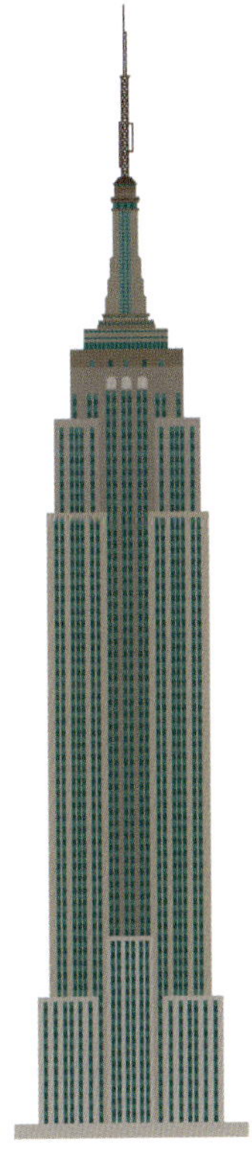

Let's head north to CANADA. Here we go!
We'll play **hockey** and **ski** in the ice and snow.
Taste **maple syrup**, view **Niagara Falls**.
Can you spot a **whale**? Can you hear **moose** calls?

11
30
21

We'll warm up in MEXICO! How bright and pretty.
Find **maracas**, **tamales**, and ruins of an **ancient city**.

Looking for **llamas**? Travel south to PERU,
and find a **sloth**, a **pan flute**, and **Machu Picchu**!

Let's visit LONDON, ENGLAND, across the sea.
Find **fish and chips** and a spot of **tea**.
Look for **Big Ben** and the **London Eye**,
then wave to the **palace** as the **bus** rides by!

TELEPHONE
Fish & chips

Next stop: PARIS, FRANCE. What a special place!
Look for the **Louvre** and its **famous face**.
Search for **crêpes** and **croissants**, then after lunch hour,
spot the **Arc de Triomphe** and the **Eiffel Tower**!

With love
from
Paris

In EGYPT, let's look for things old and new.
Search for **camels**, an **ibis**, and **beetles** too.
Spot the **Sphinx**, a **pyramid**, a **sarcophagus**,
an **ankh**, and ancient **hieroglyphs**!

Let's visit CHINA! As we tour along,
find delicious **dim sum** and a noisy **gong**.
Search for a **dragon** and **statues** so tall,
a **pagoda**, a **panda**, **bamboo**, the **Great Wall**.

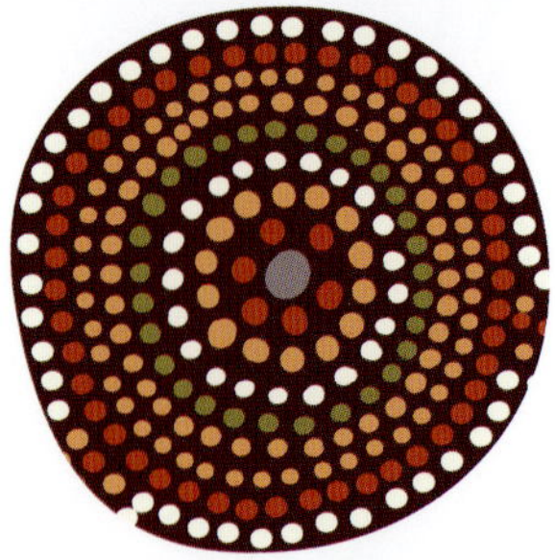

Down under in AUSTRALIA, it's time to explore.
Find the **Sydney Opera House** and a **surfer** on shore.
In the outback, search for a **kangaroo**!
Find a **platypus**, a **wombat**, and a **koala** too.

Here in JAPAN, there is **sushi** to eat,
**Mount Fuji** to climb, **cherry blossoms** so sweet.
Spot a **sumo wrestler**, downtown **Tokyo**,
**origami**, a **bonsai**, and a silk **kimono**!

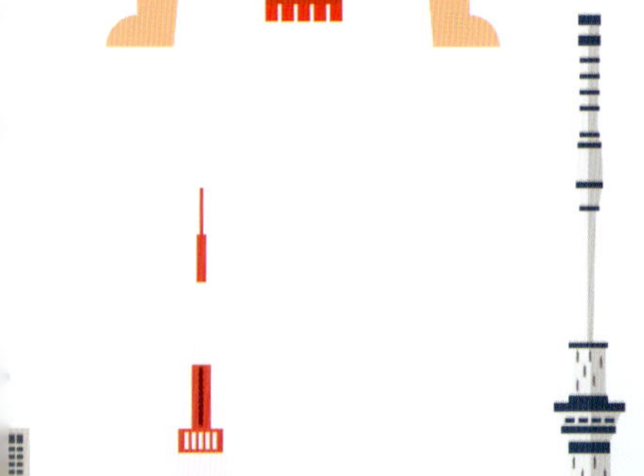

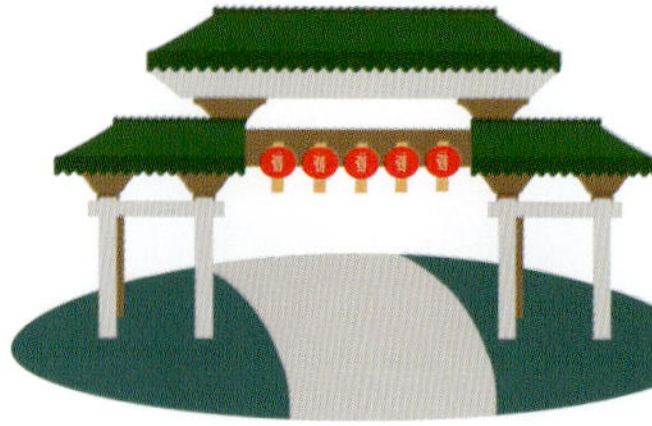

Last stop: SAN FRANCISCO. The **sea lions** are great!
Look for **Fisherman's Wharf** and the **Golden Gate**.
Find crooked **Lombard Street** and a **trolley car**.
Traveling is fun, near or far!